How Not to Sell

Sales-Support Tips For Beginners

By Brendan Shea

Stormbrew Press

©2021 Brendan Shea of Stormbrew Press
All rights reserved
This book may not be reproduced or distributed in any format without express written permission from Brendan Shea

Author's note

I have been working in sales-support for over a decade. My start was in telemarketing but I've helped manage call-centers and done some actual selling. While I've been offered higher positions in sales due to ability, my overall preference has been for sales-support.

Maybe one day I'll get into the actual selling process full-time, but according to both my personal experience and some excellent, objective DISC testing, I am pretty much right where I belong.

Someone once said that your work should involve acumen, affinity and affirmation; When one or two are present, you might be offered a role, but when all three are met, that is the trifecta.

Whatever the case, this book recounts the overall sales-support process, which intrinsically provides many rudimentary sales tips. I hope this little volume helps you. It is meant for beginners, those just getting started in sales-support.

-Brendan Shea
San Jose, California
Winter 2022

Table of Contents

Author's note

How did I get here?

Why do I want to sell things?

Why do people buy specific things?

Why don't I need to "sell"?

Who is this customer anyway?

Are they *your* customer?

How to cut bait and run

Do you know your stuff?

Do you know too much?

Should rapport be real? Yes!

Do I always try to build rapport? No

Tell me about your interest, customer

Call Control

Taking good notes

Why do you need all this information?

An accord is reached?

I want your quote!

Who is best to sell to this customer?

It matters how I schedule this quote?

Passing the baton carefully

On to the next one

About the author

How did I get here?

Sometimes people find themselves in a sales road unexpectedly. I myself had grown up in an intellectual home, with the arts figuring big in my family. After I dropped out of high school, my parents insisted I work.

I spent ten years doing everything from bussing and waiting on tables, to prepping food and eventually managing a restaurant. The management job was in New York City, where I got into acting.

The next ten years or so were taken up largely with acting, but when an illness grounded me, I had to get a job, and quickly. Telemarketing seemed a good choice. I could use my ability to think on my feet in dialoguing with customers to convey information and to sell.

Some are born salespeople, some are accidental salespeople. Once you're in a sales role, you've got to commit, or plan your road out. There are bills to pay, and you don't want to be miserable in your role; that won't work in the long run.

Sometimes, people sell something they're not sure they believe in, but if they drink the kool-aid, and realize the value of the product, then they are hooked. They might move on later to another product, but once they believe, they seldom change their feelings.

I worked for a company decades ago that supplied products to Lincoln Center in Manhattan. As a performing artist, the idea of working as a waiter near the best of the best in theater, dance and music, was an exciting and awesome prospect.

Unfortunately, the supplier seemed committed only to the bottom dollar. When I'd arrive at work to cocktail wait in the afternoon before a show, there were hotel pan racks with food trays on, cans of lit sterno underneath.

It was around 3 pm when I got in, with dinner being served in the evening. The story was that the prepared food sat out for a couple of hours with the sterno keeping it warm.

I asked my coworker how much these dinners cost, and he indicated they ran $40 each, with the patrons paying for parking and the shows as well. All in all, that seemed like a rip-off for me.

When I then waited on 1950's movie star Jane Russell, serving her a pathetic appetizer that had probably received the Sterno treatment, giving her a bill for $7.50 plus drink, she gave me such a look of disdain, that I quit that job, and found one at a homey restaurant with excellent product. I happily remained there for some time.

How you come to find yourself in a sales role is less important than what you do with it: committing, learning and growing, brings respect, reward and even peace. But if it is not for you, use it as a springboard to whatever profession brings you peace and provision.

This book contains sales knowledge gleaned in my ten years in sales-support call centers. The title concept relates to an old book on acting from decades ago. The book's title indicates that the best actors do not act at all; they are simply behaving naturally within the confines of the character they are portraying.

I am not suggesting you act when selling, but rather, that you don't need to 'sell'. When you know your product and service, believe in it, and work hard, success in sales is a natural outflow.

The chapters herein describe how to best do your job as a sales-support representative, and that by following those steps, the customer's tendency to feel comfortable and well taken care of will lead to them buying quite often when the salesperson gets them to the table.

Then, if you sense yourself growing out of that role, it can be the perfect entrée to a job in sales itself.

Why do I want to sell things?

Some people tend to manipulate to a degree, manipulators, some are about convincing customers of something; some like to explain things, and some just *believe*. If you want to manipulate, this book probably can't help you; if you want to convince, you'll have modest success; but if you are an explainer or a believer, you'll go far.

Manipulators tend to be subtle and less straightforward. When a customer feels a salesperson is trying to bait and switch, trying to pull one over on them, they will often run the other way. Sadly, some customers are duped by manipulators, but many see them coming and avoid being exploited.

I'm not saying anyone is purely a manipulator, it is a trap that can be fallen into subtly at times, but strong manipulators usually have an agenda, and it is often that the manipulators agenda trumps the customers wants and needs in too many cases.

I worked at a mortgage company in the past, where some loan officers charged more points than others, some enjoying the 'game', but seemingly still trying to provide good service.

Other loan agents would try to provide greater value, with one charging very modest points with the understanding that he'd pull in tons of deals.

He did not want to ream the clients, and had skills to bring in volume, so the head of the company gave him freedom to keep his conscience.

All these men and women were actually really decent, but when I heard of some boasting of charging several points on the back end of a loan, it kind of rankled; not that I am without flaws.

Near the end of my time there, we had a guy come in, making three times what the others made. He charged an obscene amount of points. I didn't have anything against him as a person, but he wasn't there long, and I was kind of relieved when he left.

Convincers sometimes fail because the customer senses the salesperson has an agenda and when one person is pushing, the other person is generally moving in the other direction.

These salespeople are somewhat distinct from manipulators in that they are aggressively pushing their agenda, as opposed to sneaking it past the customer's notice.

Convincers' methods are often counterproductive, whether or not they truly believe in their product or service.

Sometimes on a customer call, I try to convince the callee of my firm's value or service, or to steer them away from a competitor whose product or service I feel lacks quality.

Indicating your company's quality has some value, but again, it is better to state facts and let the customer draw their own conclusions.

Bad-mouthing a competitor who does shoddy work is usually a bad idea. Your intentions might be good, but you can create a negative atmosphere on the call.

Explainers can be annoying or helpful depending on the circumstances, but explainers are simply trying to reveal the what, why and how of things.

Explainers can be convincers and manipulators, or simply be salespeople who straightforwardly put the facts on the table.

A good explainer just turns over all the cards so the customer can see them. They assemble the puzzle and the customer sees the picture: trust is born.

I tend to overtalk or over-explain, and that is something I work to pare away at. Sometimes salespeople can explain their way into a corner. Not that they are using subterfuge, per se, but just that keeping conversations simple tends to be more enjoyable all around.

Believers are in a class by themselves, and are usually also explainers. They not only know how to present their product or service, but they are fully convinced that what they are selling is the best thing out there, and while believers do have to pay the rent, they usually have the best interests of the customer at heart. To be a true believer is to be a great salesperson.

People want to be salespeople to make money, to feel powerful, to feel empowered, to fulfill their desire to impart information in a helpful way, to make the world a better place, or all of the above. To be clear, I have not met many salespeople who were manipulators, and those I did, were not long on the scene.

Why do people buy specific things?

Manufacturers are shrewd in how they market their products. Just look at advertising; consumers are meant to feel strong, invincible, beautiful, special, unique, superior, enduring, to name a few.

They buy comforts, shelter, transportation, utility, appearance and more.

The more specific question is,

"why would someone want to buy <u>your</u> product?"

Is it less expensive? Of better quality? Longer lasting? Does it give status, attract relationships or improve retirement? Does it even bring well-being or enhance peace?

If you believe in your product but think it is not right for a specific customer, let them know! But if they want it anyway, sometimes you have to step out of their way and allow them to do what they want.

I'm not suggesting unethical practice, be upfront and honest! But I have found there are some customers for whom my products might not always be helpful, that really want to buy them regardless. Once I've shared my impression with the customer, however, it is up to them to make the decision.

Generally, The only time it would not be up to them is if the company won't allow it because it is unethical, impermissible, unsafe, or too much of a hassle. Companies have rules about these things so that they can operate safely and efficiently. If one company won't provide the work, there may be another that will, as many companies operate uniquely from others.

Sometimes it is good to have a quality referral company in your arsenal so that you can avoid upsetting your customer by helping them to reach out to another firm who will take on their project or sell them the product.

What's more, not everyone wants *your* version of the product. For example, some people who need kitchen knives purchase a set via television inexpensively. They enjoy the solution that works for them, and maybe replace them a few times.

Others buy a very high-end set of cutlery, spend a large amount to do so, enjoy the utility of those knives, and probably never have to replace them.

Neither solution is the *correct* solution; each customer has a different need, a different budget, and even customers who have large sums of money to spend, don't always go for the expensive cutlery; it's not what they want.

Ironically, sometimes even those with *less* disposable cash buy the expensive stuff because they know they're making a good investment. Everyone has a different perspective and ethos.

To the example above, my wife had a CUTCO knife salesman come over one day, and after she had talked with him for a while, she called me into the room, "They're only six easy payments of $125!", for the selection of knives she wanted to purchase.

"Seven hundred and fifty dollars?!" I gasped, doing the math.

"You and your numbers. There's even a veggie knife for when you make your pasta sauce." She had secured my stake in her culinary plot.

I relented, seeing the value. I knew how good CUTCO was: incredible action of the blade, handles big enough for the hand to grip, composite hand-holds with carbon steel, full-tang, and a lifetime guarantee.

We were both hooked. Working class folks.

Sure, we could have purchased Ginsu, Wusthof or something in between, but we've had our knives for ten years, and we'll probably never have a reason to replace them… just to buy more…

Why don't I need to "sell"?

Many enter the world of sales, convinced that persuasion is part of the game. They are right, it is part of the game... for some... for others, it is a matter of saying enough words that the customer is exhausted to the point of capitulation, and they'll do anything to end the dialogue (not necessarily buying your product).

There are salespeople who understand that meeting a person, whether face to face, over the phone or online, listening to what they have to say[1], and then responding accordingly, is the road to buying. You thought I'd say the road to selling? The road to their being ready to buy is what I mean.

---

[1] Listening is easier said than done when you have an agenda; even if the agenda is on their behalf.

When a customer is already interested in your product, but is not assured of your company's price, comportment[2], competency, efficiency or service, your job is not necessarily to convince them you are superior to others in those areas[3], but rather to state how *you* operate in those areas, and to give valid and easy to follow proof.

Then, the customer is not on the defensive, and can say what they have been dying to say, "Yes!".

There is a story about counterfeiting and the Canadian Mounted Police in which the mounties were trained by close inspection of real currency only. When fake currency was later encountered, it stood out like a sore thumb because it was different from what they had studied.

---

[2] Behavior
[3] Given, it can be an easy trap to talk away about how you are better than the others

As noted before, telling the customer how bad other companies are is a trap that is easy to fall into, particularly if it is true. I've caught myself doing it. Try to focus on what you do well, and then let the customer decide on what they want.

Who is this customer anyway?

So, who am I speaking to here?

I work on the phone, qualifying customers, gathering data, and setting sales appointments...

When I talk to a customer, my first job is to:

A. Understand their overall personality type
B. Recognize their mood and availability to talk
C. Inform them of my process to ensure it works for them

Otherwise, we both waste valuable time when later discoveries preclude working together (I'll explain more shortly)

Sometimes I realize who this person is right away:

A. They are assertive or aggressive
B. They are succinct[4]
C. They need to explain everything in detail

---

[4] Brief and to the point/Uses few words

D. They are subtle
E. They are outgoing
F. They like to talk
G. They need to know they are heard

Once I know what their communication style is like, I can gear my communication accordingly. People who don't like a lot of detail will appreciate a salesperson who sticks to the facts. Others, who think out loud *may* want their salesperson to talk them through all the specifics.

If the customer is in a rush and I need more of their time, I pivot and offer to reconnect later. I find it frustrating to get partway through my process and have the customer drop-out to attend another meeting.

Yes, I want to then complete the conversation I'm having, but I'd rather get everything established with regard to the appointment, and usually my clients feel the same. Those who do try to rush things usually find they are confused, and stressed, as their next impending meetings loom, and they often decide to reconvene anyway, or they abandon our mutual endeavor altogether.

Once it is established that there is time to talk, I also let the customer know that our company has certain parameters on deliverables[5], so that the customer doesn't spend a lot of time with me only to find that my company is going to take too long, charge too much or fall short of the customer's non-negotiable criteria in some manner.

If there is no such issue, then we are ready to talk.

---

[5] Products and services

Are they *your* customer?

James Thompson spoke with the salesman from the widget company. James wanted widgets sized one millimeter larger than that company's selection at that scale.

Rhonda Craig cared about nothing but paying the very lowest price. The salesman talked about quality, durability, service; he might as well have been talking to a brick.

Every customer is not *your* customer. Not everyone who looks into your firm is going to set an appointment, and not all people you quote will buy from you. As a sales support rep, what you need to recognize to a degree, is, are they 'your company's customer'?

How do you determine that? You might want to try one of the following:

A.   Find out if they are shopping for the lowest price
B.   See if they want you to give them all the answers before the quote

C.   Understand if they are patient with processes

A.   If they just want the lowest price, you'll probably know if they are your customer or not. If your company's priority is simply the bottom line price, then you're in good shape, but if your firm spends more on quality and service, then your price may be higher, and you'll want to tell the customer up front, to avoid wasting time. Wasted time in sales is usually wasted for all parties.

B.   If they don't want a lot of information about your company, then they might or might not be your customer, depending on your company's way of doing business, or unless they want your company to handle the granular details. Again, your particular services and business model are key to this category.

C.   If your company has careful processes and the customer is not patient with how you work to ensure the project is managed correctly, that could present a problem, but if the company is free to work according to their own business model, there should be no problem.

On the other hand, some customers are so intent on careful procedure that they hinder the process. Most companies don't turn away such customers, but these buyers don't make for good sales success stories and can be a hindrance to themselves, their projects and their firms.

How to cut bait and run

When you find out that a customer is unqualified, too aggressive, too detail oriented, or just not nice, you may still have to deal with them. In some cases, however, you may be able to appropriately cut bait and run.

Some conversations with customers do not go well, and the best way to cut bait and run is simply to acknowledge to the customer that your price may be too high, your company may not be able to provide the type of service they are wanting, or just to respond in whatever polite, diplomatic and honest way possible, to convey your lack of assurance for the process.

Some companies might frown on a 'cut bait and run' philosophy, but others see the need to promote an equality in business stature, preserving the sanity and character of all parties. Good business is predicated on mutual respect.

Still, overall, these types of situations can be delicate matters. Sometimes the customer takes the work off of your hands by saying something like:

A.   You guys seem to be priced too high for what you are selling

B.   your timeline for the project is not in line with my plans

C.   I appreciate your attention to detail, but I just want to get this thing going

And at those times, it is easy to cut bait and run, because you don't have what they want and hopefully they will realize that and not be upset; after all, as with any relationship, some work better than others.

When it is not easy to cut bait, just tread carefully so as not to offend. That customer will be better served by another company that operates in a way more conducive to that customer's preferences.

You are doing them a favor by being honest with them about how you see their ask[6] relative to your offerings. If you do set an appointment with them, it is up to the sales staff to take the reins. Time will tell whether the customer comes into the fold.

---

[6] An "ask" in Sales parlance is basically a request

Do you know your stuff?

It is important to know your company, product, service, customer and industry as best you can. This takes time, and rather than make up baloney answers when you don't know how to respond to a question, tell your customer the item is new to you or is complex, and that you'll look into it with senior staff and get them an answer.

Customers can smell a fake a mile away, and making up an answer while tempting, is unethical at worst and unprofessional at best. Most people will understand your need to inquire. No one knows everything so you are in good company.

When I started in telemarketing, I kind of glossed over some things once or twice. I'm not proud of it. I didn't misrepresent the facts per se, but if I didn't know something, I acted like I was informed beyond what was true. Fortunately for my moral and ethical conscience, that did not persist.

Someone was gracious and righteous to guide me. They said my best strategy was to note the questions, tell the customer I had done that, and promise to have someone more knowledgeable answer with clarity and authority.

It is said a person who admits he or she is ignorant on a subject, is in fact more informed than the person who pretends to know something when they don't; they are the ignorant ones.

Here is a short laundry list of some key items you must begin to study as soon as you can:

1. Company History
2. Product
3. Software
4. Pricing
5. Customer demographic
6. Industry/Trends
7. Technicals

The more you know, the better able you'll be to guide your customer through the maze of the sales support process. And remember, knowledge takes time.

Do you know too much?

I can know too much? In a sense you can. Sales is a numbers game, and while *relationship* is often key, there are two things that hinder the sales process for all; these are to be carefully avoided:

1.   "Throwing up" knowledge on the customer

I had been a telemarketer for a few years when I was offered to do some customer 'facing' phone sales, by my then company.

The more I learned, the more I wanted to tell the customer; I still struggle with this today. My manager at a sales training for the sales work I was to do, emphasized several times to not' throw up on the customer.

The trainer was the head of sales at the company, and his ideas seemed radical to me; sometimes, I thought they were slightly unethical. But when I look back, he was imploring us to not share buckets of data.

When a head coach in the NFL wins a Superbowl, someone sneaks up behind him and dumps a cooler of gatorade on them in admiration to celebrate the moment.

But when a salesperson dumps a bucket of data on a customer in a monologue that denies a good dialogue, the customer might feel like they've been violated.

I've had customers violate me emotionally, and it is *not* fun. My sales manager was wise in his admonition, and as this issue is still something I struggle with, looking back, I definitely appreciate him for it.

2. Showing that you know a lot more than is required to accomplish your stage of the process

a. This is a trap very easily fallen into when explaining things to a customer

b. Try to continually find ways to explain things in truncated form

c.   Try to explain things in single sentences not paragraphs

d.   Use single word answers when possible

e.   If the customer jumps into this process with you, find ways to move on politely

f.   Remember, if you take too long with one customer, you'll potentially be failing others

g.   Further, if you provide such customized service to one customer that your company suffers, your existing clients may suffer as well

h.   Like me, you may not be the center of the company, but as a cog in the wheel, your smooth operation is being counted on; keep that in mind.

(more on this subject later on in: [Call control](#))

Should rapport be real? Yes!

Here is where sales can become fun. Sales is fun? I have found myself on the phone with customers who've lived somewhere I've lived, are involved in a line of work I find fascinating or have had a similar experience as me. It is at those times that I am inclined to speak up.

I might let the customer know of the commonality, in a low-key way, so as not to offend them. I don't want to disturb the professionalism of the interaction, as the customer may not be inclined to chat about their old neighborhood, line of work, or whatever.

At such times, I get a feel for the person according to earlier chapters in this book, and if they seem easygoing, I make a comment or two. Building rapport can be a good way to break the ice when a customer is unsure of how the company they are reaching out to operates. It is also just a good way to be friendly.

Rapport should always be real: If you're not really a Tom Hanks fan (I am), and you mention that he grew up near where you lived in Oakland (he did), then you might not want to touch on that bit of trivia.

You also don't want to name drop. I've met a lot of stars as I was a waiter in New York City. Does it mean anything that I met all these people? It does to me, I was an actor, but in the larger scheme of things, name dropping to build rapport, or boasting of an accomplishment, these are easily done, but can sour a conversation.

If the callee brings something up that you identify with, and you can bring something interesting to the table, by all means, that might be good, but otherwise, try to not be 'over-knowledgeable'; everyone knows a lot, but not everyone shares their knowledge compulsively.

Finally, don't use rapport to make a sale, use rapport to improve the conversation, and if it works, allow the improved relationship to make the customer feel better about talking with you. Sales can be a transient interaction, so you might not make a close friend, but you might make someone's day, and that should make you feel good.

Do I *always* try to build rapport? *No*

As we went over in "Who is this customer…?" and "Are they your customer?", not all customers think and act the same, and not all customers want the same kind of treatment.

Many customers I've talked with over the years are referred to in sales parlance[7] with words similar to "Cobra" or "Powerhouse", while some customers are just succinct, and not necessarily overtly aggressive.

In my experience, these customers do not require the following at all:

1. Boilerplate[8] marketing spiels about your company, product or service
2. Your own opinions about the deliverables
3. Any personal chit chat or rapport building

---

[7] A Way of speaking particular to a specific job field
[8] Written Marketing materials, that can be spoken out, routinely describing your product or service

When you identify the customer as aggressive, assertive, and specifically as succinct, don't bother trying to build rapport with them; instead, give them the facts, answer their questions to the letter, and get them to the next step in the process.

You don't need to cower before them or be afraid, and they will also respect you for keeping things simple.

Also, just because a customer is not assertive, don't assume that rapport building is OK. If you say something to build rapport and it falls flat, leave it there and move right on.

Even the gentle and the chatty customers have their limits; after a while you'll get to know whom you can talk with on a rapport building level and whom you shouldn't.

A note of caution: even good rapport can backfire if the customer wants to chit chat too much; you have other calls to make, and you need to move on to the next customer.

As with Chapter 3: "Why do people buy specific things", it's good to draw the customer out of their shell. If they say they want a certain project timeline, brand or method of acquisition, it's sometimes good to ask them, "*Why?*"

If they are taken aback by any questions you ask, let them know that your motive is not to disqualify them as a customer, not to question their judgment, nor to imply they should go with financing over cash (for example).

Once you understand the "Why", you are better able to move the conversation to the next steps in the best manner. This is one of countless examples of why *listening* is often considered a lost art, so important and rare is it, and so difficult to maintain when you have an agenda[9].

---

[9] Because a salesperson has an agenda doesn't necessarily mean their agenda isn't customer-centric

You won't always have to draw out the customer's 'Why'. Sometimes, they'll tell you in an aggressive manner, or just make it plain in a low-key way. If they are aggressive, be sure to be politely assertive as well, don't crumble.

You let them know if you can deliver what they are asking for in the why. If they just state it, you respond in kind, and again, tell them how your company approaches the item they are asking for, or if they are aggressive, just tell them that should work and move forward with the call.

The 'Why' is important to convey to the salesperson so that they understand more about how the customer ticks; understanding the customer's personality type and motivation means the salesperson can have in mind what is key to their customer.

When the meeting or appointment occurs later with the salesperson, the "table" is well-set for all involved. When the salesperson and the customer are "at the table", having the elements of the meal well in place, allows the salesperson to do their job with fewer distractions.

The why, is one of the 'Settings' involved in a well-arranged sales meeting.

Tell me about your interest, customer

As with Chapter 3: "Why do people buy specific things", it's good to draw the customer out of their shell. If they say they want a certain project timeline, brand or method of acquisition, it's sometimes good to ask them, *"Why?"*

If they are taken aback by any questions you ask, let them know that your motive is not to disqualify them as a customer, not to question their judgment, nor to imply they should go with financing over cash (for example).

Once you understand the "Why", you are better able to move the conversation to the next steps in the best manner. This is one of countless examples of why <u>*listening*</u> is often considered a lost art, so important and rare is it, and so difficult to maintain when you have an agenda[10].

---

[10] Because a salesperson has an agenda doesn't necessarily mean their agenda isn't customer-centric

You won't always have to draw out the customer's 'Why'. Sometimes, they'll tell you in an aggressive manner, or just make it plain in a low-key way. If they are aggressive, be sure to be politely assertive as well, don't crumble.

You let them know if you can deliver what they are asking for in the why. If they just state it, you respond in kind, and again, tell them how your company approaches the item they are asking for, or if they are aggressive, just tell them that should work and move forward with the call.

The 'Why' is important to convey to the salesperson so that they understand more about how the customer ticks; understanding the customer's personality type and motivation means the salesperson can have in mind what is key to their customer.

When the meeting or appointment occurs later with the salesperson, the "table" is well-set for all involved. When the salesperson and the customer are "at the table", having the elements of the meal well in place, allows the salesperson to do their job with fewer distractions.

The why, is one of the 'Settings' involved in a well-arranged sales meeting.

Call control

I've talked a lot about listening. That sounds like an oxymoron, but seriously, there are two key elements to a sales support appointment setting conversation:

A. Listening
B. Call Control

So it's super important to listen, but if you are setting appointments and need to get to the next call, you also need to control the call.

I love to build rapport by walking with customers through a joint process of dialoguing, where I think, reply, and act, based on what the customer and I are talking about. When we are done, there can be a good working relationship in which both parties can feel the time was well spent and effective, pleasant even.

Still, especially if you are in Sales-Support like me, you do have to call other customers. Sales is a numbers game, so the more people you reach out to, the more you get ahold of, the more appointments you set, and the more jobs typically sell.

But process is important, so if you "run roughshod" over a customer to set the bid and move on, you may hurt the salesperson's chances and offend the customer.

Where is the balance between process-oriented communication which builds rapport, and efficient communication which increases your bottom-line for appointments set in a given period? That is probably up to your company and you. It is up to your company to set statistical expectations and review KPI's[11] and it is up to you to navigate them.

---

[11] Key Performance Indicators (metrics)

Insofar as it is up to you, try to run or obtain reports indicating how many of your appointments sell, and under what circumstances. Some companies will tell you how many hours you spend talking on the phone.

Your company's software can help you to determine these figures. Then you can see what length of call yields the best results.

Another important aspect of call-control is customer-centric: There are other customers who've inquired, and they want to hear from you.

You may have to do any or all of the following:

1. Reply to texts
2. Reply to emails
3. Reply to voicemails
4. reply to web-inquiries

And there may be a ton of inquiries each day.

Customers will only wait so long to speak with you before they move on. You'll want to respond to each and every one of them in a timely way. Insofar as it is possible, you'll want to reply promptly and thoroughly. Depending on supply and demand of staffing and customers, this can be challenging.

You want to help your customers, and you also don't want to receive a poor review if you are unable to reach out in time. This is not always within your control, but as much as it is, make it a priority.

One time, I worked in an era where my company was deluged with new business, and we were not able to bring in enough new help to immediately accommodate the inflow, so we had to be as efficient as humanly possible while still providing good service.

A good problem to have, but... stressful.

Taking good notes

I love taking extensive project notes. Sometimes I probably overdo it. I will say that 'underdoing' it can be a problem in sales and project management. Some projects are very straightforward, requiring only the most basic appointment notes, but others are very complex, or in some cases, the clients provide a *lot* of information.

Do you include all of what the client mentioned? It might depend on you, them, the company, the salesperson you are setting the bid for, and the product. If the product or service involves technology or engineering, basically, anything complex, including thorough notes is helpful.

Also, be sure to get their contact information and address letter-perfect; nothing is worse than a missed appointment, or a confused customer who fails to receive a timely email or other communication.

Can I leave some information out?

If you're building rapport with the customer and they say they used to run a tech giant, you should include that for sure. They don't need to be VIP's either; any information that helps the sales rep understand the lay of the land can be useful, but if the customer goes on about non-project related items (no offense, I do too sometimes!), don't feel like you have to take dictation; use your judgment.

How should I take the notes?

Pen and paper are fine, but I'm a big fan of **Microsoft OneNote**. OneNote provides digital notepads with folders, tabs and subjects; When a customer calls in to my desk, I often need to take notes immediately, before I can create a record in my CRM[12].

I create notes in OneNote, and my gain is:

---

[12] Customer Relationship Management; (CRM is a customer database from which companies can store customer records, appointment data, project data and much more. CRM's can be simplistic or vastly complex

1. Notes that can be taken quickly
2. Neat legible notes
3. Notes organized by subject
4. Notes that can be pasted elsewhere
5. Notes that can be emailed directly
6. No wasted paper
7. No need to store notes physically

Once it is clear the caller wants an appointment, I can paste any relevant data to and from CRM.

Good, concise notes, as is probably obvious, have the following benefit:

1. Provide a written record for future inquiry
2. Help you to be organized and aid in recall
3. Give the sales rep a clear picture of scenario
4. Help the customer have their needs met

Keeping your notes clear and precise provides your salesperson with helpful information they'll appreciate.

Why do you need all this information?

Many customers you talk with will not understand why you need a lot of information from them. Not all industries require tons of information for a quote.

When I worked in the mortgage industry decades ago, we had to gain the customers' trust to the degree that they submitted their social security numbers in full.

Later, I started in the solar industry around 2011, customers were suspicious that we needed their electric history! It wasn't as if we were asking to see their bank accounts or read their personal journals.

Fortunately, today, most solar consumers get that installers need kWh usage in order to size systems correctly, so there has been some progress, but even today, many folks are unaware that a solar installation is similar to other construction projects whose accurate design is predicated on the analysis of considerable data.

We recently had a sales rep come to our home from a construction outfit to bid on some work, and with a few quick questions, some measurements and an iPad, the guy was in and out of our home in half an hour, having quoted the job. This quote was just for windows, and was fairly simple.

Some sales calls are simple and some are very technical. For the latter, explain to your customer the reasons for needing the data. Let them know you have no interest in their private information, but that in order to properly assess their need, the data is key.

You can also tell them that you don't want to sell them the wrong amount of equipment, or the wrong items altogether.

State upfront that while you are naturally in the business of selling things, you want to be consultative, and desire they have a good outcome.

Tell them the truth: If they have a good outcome, they'll refer more business to you. Being honest and forthcoming should earn you the respect of most customers, and if you lose a few, they weren't meant to work with your company in the first place.

Of course, you should **always** be honest, but if you are new to the company, be sure your *style* of communication is appropriate. I've been selling for years, so I'm confident in *most* conversations.

Once they understand the data you need is for *their* benefit, they may be more willing to share it.

I've worked for companies where we needed a customers':

1. Electric history
2. Loan to Value[13]
3. Borrowing preferences
4. Social Security number
5. Home address
6. Contact information
7. Time and attention
8. Overall trust and confidence

As a sales-support person, you'll need to obtain some things from this list, you'll probably need to glean many of these items. Don't be intimidated by them; earn the customer's trust, be matter of fact that information is needed, and you'll probably do fine.

---

[13] What a lender will loan, based on mortgage divided by value of home

In this age of identity theft, most people won't and shouldn't give out their social security number, but as I mentioned, years ago, when I was getting started in sales, we had to obtain that information for each and every one of our customers before they could go to the next step in our company's process. Times have changed.

An accord is reached?

When you get on the phone with a prospective customer[14], you'll need to let them know how your company operates with regard to quotes, to ensure they are on board (we covered that in "Who is this customer anyway?").

An initial accord[15] is then reached, but later, when you are asking for their information, as noted in the last chapter, they may raise objections. Or, there may be complications:

1. They don't have the data you need
2. They don't understand what you are asking for
3. They aren't in agreement with you as to the nature of the data
4. There is a communication problem

---

[14] Sometimes known as a Lead
[15] An agreement

At this point, you may have to sacrifice some of your normal parameters to get the job of setting an appointment done, or, you may have to tell them you need to check in with your manager to ensure you can quote them accurately.

Diplomacy is key here. You don't want to upset the customer. Customers can be cranky sometimes, and so can employees; be sure to maintain courtesy and professionalism at all times.

Anyone can get frustrated, and it is your job to keep things cool. Do what you can, and if setting the appointment (or selling the job) needs to wait until you have consulted with a higher up, then understand that sometimes occurs and try not to annoy the customer when conveying that fact.

Try to keep in agreement; if they are frustrated, sympathize, be in agreement with them, and do your best to meet their requests. Don't violate company policy or model, but see if there is a bridge between your company's protocol and the customer's request. can. This is something a salesperson must sometimes grapple with.

If you are new, let the customer know that, and tell them to ensure you handle their project correctly, you'd like to get a manager's opinion. Let them know you are in their corner, and go from there.

As noted, there will occasionally be times when you have a customer you just can't please, and on those occasions, all you can do is be polite, firm, and move on. This can be difficult, and experience is the best teacher.

I want your quote!

At some point, if things go well, the customer will often want a quote. Once you have their information, it is important to get them scheduled right away, as soon as you can; if they absolutely do not qualify, tell them politely, but remember, people buy things for their own reasons.

Don't take advantage of them, but as was said before, don't stand in their way if they want to buy; it is their choice, not yours. Advise them, and then let them decide.

I have had customers tell me in the first five minutes of a call that they are not only going to set the appointment, but that they will only buy from our company.

Conversely, I've had situations where a customer interviewed me about my company's product and service for a *long* time.

Again, satisfying the customers initial concerns up front is important. Defining your appointment setting parameters equally so. Meeting in the middle is ideal, but all calls are different and your call control skills will become more nuanced as time goes on.

Who is best to sell to this customer?

It is important to know your sales rep staff. They are unique men and women with their own special qualities. While all may be excellent salespeople, some may be better suited than others, to sell to a particular customer.

In, "Who is this customer anyway?", we examined what makes customers tick; in this chapter, I want to point out that matching the customer with the right sales rep is also key.

I can't recall working at any jobs where there was favoritism with assignments, and am very glad of that. When assigning sales reps to appointments, equal distribution is key.

That being said, playing "matchmaker" is not a bad thing, as long as all reps get equal opportunity!

1. Do you have a customer who hates to waste time?
a. Match them with an efficient rep
2.

3. Does this customer like to talk everything out?
a. pair them with someone like-minded

Sometimes opposites attract, but following the above should bring about better results most of the time, and I've even told customers that I'm matching them with a rep who is suited to the task; from what the customers are telling me, they are pleased with this method.

It matters how I schedule this quote?

Now that you have a sales rep in mind for the customer, you must schedule them; why is this so important? Each rep has their own set of criteria, personal calendar events, and more. Also, while appointments often are set at preset intervals, some clients require more time while some don't want to dally.

When scheduling a bid, be sure the rep has time for the following (as applicable to your company)

1. Family
2. Meals
3. Travel
4. Restroom
5. Personal Appointments
6. Vacations
7. Holidays

By caring for both customer and sales rep, you ensure a happy customer, *and* a happy salesperson, who has less likelihood of burning out. In your company you must remember that you're all in this together, so think like a team!

Passing the baton carefully

Now you've come to the salesworld, made a commitment, learned about the product, technology and customer, figured out how to communicate about the project, product or service, and carefully assigned and calendared the appointment.

Now, you must carefully pass the baton to the salesperson by following these or similar steps:

1. Place correct information on rep's calendar
2. Email rep and customer of appointment
3. Request any needed data of customer
4. Fill out any requisite paperwork
5. Inform rep of any special customer information
6. Ensure all CRM data is correct and saved
7. Log any applicable future action items
8. Monitor emails, texts and voicemails for updates
9. Store inbound data as required
10. Email management of any special requests

By following above or similar steps particular to your company, you'll ensure proper carryover of customers from your sales-support oversight, to the sales rep's purview.

From there, it is up to the rep to manage things carefully, but if you have 'set the table' carefully, the rep should be able to serve the 'meal', making their presentation and dialoguing with the customer to see if there is a good fit.

On to the next one

Each customer is very important, as a person, as a project-related individual, and as a potential revenue source. I don't mean that they are just dollar signs to salespeople; customers are not only our bread and butter, but individuals with lives, work and families of their own.

Still, once a sales-support rep finishes working with one customer, as with most professions, she or he must go right on to the next one. An email comes in, the phone rings, or a text chimes. Reps need breaks, days off, and vacations, but the next customer is usually just around the corner.

Take good care of yourself, your reps and your customers. You'll be needing to earn money for many years, unless you hit the lottery, inherit millions, or fall into some other unusual fortune. Enjoy your life in sales-support; it can be very rewarding.

Acknowledgements

There are a lot of circumstances that brought me into sales, good and bad, but if it had not been for God's help, my family's teaching and my colleagues inestimable help, I'd never have established myself in sales-support nor gained the knowledge of the field and appreciation of the work that I have.

With that in mind, I'd like to thank my mom, my grandfather, my sister, Michelle B., Patrick, Danette, Gene, Christine, John N., Kevin G., Gentry, Brian, Scott A., Robin B., Chris C., Tyler N., Shelley M., Misty, Tom M., and a very special shout to all of the crew at my current job.

About the author

Brendan Shea is a veteran sales-support representative. Shea has worked on both coasts in a number of different industries with different products, and feels there is a straightforward path to sales success:

Find a product you feel confident about and proud of, and then find a company that evokes similar sentiment, trusting your gut and checking out the company's way of doing business. Then, when working for them, "selling" is not really a thing.

Selling will not be without challenges, but anyone can learn to sell. Not that everyone would want to, "If you don't like selling, don't sell; dig a ditch, star in a film, become a personal chef, become an accountant, paint a painting." In short, do what you love and love what you do.

www.ingramcontent.com/pod-product-compliance
Lightning Source LLC
Chambersburg PA
CBHW052337220526
45472CB00001B/466

9798479190629